# Bedtime Stories for Capitalists

Sky Lucas    Jeff Hamer
Illustrated by Sam Keiser

Discobolos

ISBN:    978-0-9973523-0-6

Library of Congress Control Number:    2016903369

Bedtime Stories for Capitalists

Library of Congress Cataloging-in-Publication Data

Hamer, Jeffrey M. (1949— ) and Lucas, Sky M. (1957— )

Second printing, 2016

o  o

Special discounts are available on quantity purchases by corporations, associations, educators, and others. For details, for ordering information, for information regarding permissions to reproduce selections, or U.S. trade bookstores and wholesalers, contact Asset Direction Incorporated:

info@assetdirectioninc.com
001 815 361 7577

The primary text of this book is composed in 12 point Palatino Linotype.
The display text of this book is composed in 24 point Segoe Script.
Design and composition by Asset Direction Incorporated.

Manufactured and Printed in the United States of America

Discobolos Publishing Company
4607 Lakeview Canyon Road Suite 104
Westlake Village CA 91361 USA

*H*ush little baby, don't say a word, Daddy's
gonna buy you a mockingbird...

*And if that mockingbird won't sing,*
*Daddy's gonna buy you a diamond ring...*

*And if that diamond ring's not there,*
*Daddy'll say, 'Get over it, life's not fair'...*

*For Harry and Norma, who sacrificed so their sons might not.*

*For my four beautiful children, Tain, Skye, Keir, Star,*
*Partners in birth and life,*
*My joy that you are close and always will be there for each other.*

*The last book I wrote was dedicated to my family: Deborah, Stephen, Jonathan and ?
My wife and sons made (and make) life meaningful.*

*Now "little question mark" gets hers. To my daughter Jacqueline, with whom I've had the pleasure of triangulating the rest of the family into misadventures from the Grand Canyon Rim-to-Rim and into the mouth of an erupting volcano...*

*These are stories about investing.*

*It is said that parents transition—in their children's eyes—from (at first) infallible gods, to (next, in teenage years) complete idiots, and then, finally, into simply one more traveler on the road of life—but an experienced one. One who knows, and can warn, where most of the potholes are—because they fell into them.*

*So too it is along the road of investing. We wish the lessons in these stories were a result of our wisdom, but unfortunately most of them are a result of our experience. Your challenge, dear reader, is to make them part of your wisdom before they are part of your experience.*

*It is impossible to name all those who helped us acquire that experience, not to mention those whose pearls of wisdom we've simply expropriated. Nevertheless Stephen Hamer, Deborah Hamer, Eric Xia, Bill Feingold and Lawrence Cavanagh deserve special thanks. In addition Jonathan Hamer, Jacqueline Hamer, Marc Hamer, Jeff Lewis, Steve Weir, Ched Reeder, Jay Lucas, David Campbell, Tom Madsen, Nelson Donegan and John Walsh.*

# Caveman Joe

Talking heads on TV (and we humans in general) see causality everywhere, but usually it's just correlation. Breaking news: New Study shows 99% of terminal hospital patients had eaten lettuce in the past month. Obviously we must avoid lettuce.

"False Causality" happens with we Humans. Everywhere. All the time. Its foundation lies in a vital link in our evolution.

We take you to a beautiful forest, perhaps millions of years ago.

Caveman Joe and you are sitting on a log, telling jokes...

> *"Ugh!"*
> *"Hahahaha!"*
> *"UGGH!"*

and passing the time.

You might even put your clubs down beside you and take an enjoyable little nap.

Unfortunately this log is in the middle of a field... a saber tooth tiger's favorite hunting area.

There goes Joe, off to lunch.

It will be a cold day in you-know-where before you sit on that log—or any like it—ever again.

As a result, you are less likely to "do lunch" with tigers. Your association confers higher odds that you will live a long and happy life, have many children, and pass along that gene that helped you to believe that "A" causes "B".

All good so far. Those of us that have made it this far in the Big Genetic Lottery are "pre-programmed" to believe in Causality wherever we see it. It helped made us successful as a species.

Today.

You and your buddy Joe. Sitting not on a log but in the dugout at Wrigley Field. Despite all odds you are professional baseball players. (Who would have thought?)

Our pitcher Phil has a no hitter going. Ninth inning. Joe has worn his hat upside down for the past three innings. You've not uncrossed your legs, although a painful thing, for the last four... and... Yes! Phil does get that no hitter. Everyone can rejoice in the cave!

If you interview Joe later and ask, "Did you really believe wearing your hat like that would effect the outcome?" Joe replies, "I know. I know. But it just made me feel better."

You probably don't even have to think hard for examples where people believe in Causality far more than this.

Our evolution has programmed us to see Causality everywhere. Our very survival —the ability to make it to this day—depended on it. Sometimes extremely well-justified (eating poisonous mushrooms comes to mind). Other times utterly foolish.

Reliably separating logs that might kill us from logs that are safe is a useful but subtler skill. Better to stay alive first by avoiding logs altogether. The subtlety may be more important to survival on the floor of the New York Stock Exchange, but we just haven't been there very long, evolutionarily speaking.

Give us a few hundred million years there and we've no doubt those of us financially still alive at that time will be very good at it.

# Lists of Winners !

Man receives an envelope in the mail. Inside, typewritten, the single sentence: "Bet on Detroit." No return address. Into the wastebasket it goes.

Next week the same, but this time "Bet on Miami." A football fan, he recalls Detroit just won big. He keeps the letter. Sure enough, a Dolphin win next weekend. Fascinating.

Eagerly awaits the mail. A new wrinkle: "Bet on Chicago. If you want more, send $500." Complete with wire instructions! Fair enough, he thinks, phoning first his bookie then his bank.

So it goes. An astonishing five more weeks. Each, the wire account changes, the money demanded increases—beyond all reason—but so do his bets.

Week eight now is insane. After mortgaging his home to wire off half a million dollars, he settles in front of the TV to savor Dallas' win.

The Cowboys lose!

As he flees the country—barely ahead of his wife's attorneys and his bookie's enforcers—authorities find a man in a prison cell with a typewriter, friends outside, and knowledge of mathematics apparently better than our hapless hero: send 1024 letters (half on each team), next week (to the 512 winners) each half again, and so on.

Before we smugly chuckle at our fictional (perhaps) man's naivete (we'd never be that stupid) ...consider.

We all like winners. We screen investments based on track record. We don't consider the difference between luck and skill. Not because we're stupid (well, actually, because we're stupid, but not *only* because we're stupid). It's also because separating luck from skill is difficult.

There are many lists of winners. Every financial magazine worth its salt, ordinary magazines, investment services, all produce lists. They are easy to produce. But how many "winners" would there be simply as a result of luck?

Take mutual funds. A list of the 100 or so which not only beat the market for five years, but also every individual year of those five years, is an exclusive club. Impressive club. Until one realizes simply tossing a coin each year should have produced more than three times as many members.

Mutual fund managers produce performance worse than luck would predict. Reliably. Every year. Part of that is transaction costs and of course management fees. But not all. Sad fact is, the average manager actually manages to subtract value even before expenses. It's why decades of honest financial advisers suggest the average person put their money in index funds and go play golf.

Why don't the winner lists disclose this? We don't know, but we suspect it may have something to do with the fact that, *"100 Funds That Beat The Market Each And Every Year!"* just might sell a few more copies than, *"100 Funds: 10 Skilled, 90 Lucky! Guess Which? We Don't Know!"*

"Aha" we think. Does this not apply to hedge funds, commodity pools, real estate limited partnerships, etc.? Indeed it does. Does it also mean the average investor should shun them? Perhaps. Even if so, what to do?

The bad news: it's impossible to know with 100% certainty. The good news: it's possible to know with some degree of confidence. More bad news: it's not super-easy. Statistics is required. Some of us may recall hoary terms like "confidence interval". Others (our name withheld to protect the guilty) regret sleeping through our first exposure and had to study it again.

For the rest of us mortals, when looking for "lists of winners" go beyond the cover of the magazine. A few (very few, but even a few free ones) take care to stress test track records in detail. Statistical tests, Up and Down markets separately, etc.

Also there are procedural ways. One is called "Out-Of-Sample" testing. When testing an idea, we try to find something that works on a database covering a long time. But not the longest time for which we have data. We take some of the history and "hide" it from ourselves. When we're done—when we think our idea is ready to produce pots of money for us—only then do we let it try on data its never seen before. Usually we cry a lot after that and go out for a beer.

But models which survive this and other torments—we like to joke that if you torture the numbers long enough, they will confess to anything—have in our opinion a fighting chance of containing a bit of the Holy Grail: the elusive Causality.

# Euclid v. Einstein !

## "Rumble in the Jungle", Wall Street Style...

In one corner, Euclid. Sometimes called Euclid of Alexandria, he was a mathematician who lived in Egypt. He is often referred to as the Father of Geometry. References suggest that he was born mid 400 BC and died mid 300 BC. Not a bad life span by our simple math!

In the other corner, Albert Einstein. We know much more about him. Famous for theoretical physics. Other than mathematical curiosity, Albert had little interest in money. But even one of his passing observations is famous and one of our most valuable financial quotes, "Compound interest is the Eighth Wonder of the World. He who understands it, earns it. He who does not, pays it."

We're not sure who was smarter, but no matter. Let's get on with the fight. The bout is ten rounds: we'll measure their performance over a 10 year period. When these gentlemen meet (H.G. Wells generously lends his Time Machine for the event) sparks fly. The Smackdown begins.

They each have their own "money machine". Euclid chooses a fast mathematical thoroughbred: up 60% one year, down only 40% the next. Einstein picks a pokey nag capable of but half a percent each year. Doesn't look good for Albert. Each begin with a dollar (a lot of money back then). Einstein declines the coin toss; Euclid gets the head start, letting him make 60% the first year. The starting gun... Bang!

At the end of Year One it looks over before it's begun. Euclid's $1.00 has become $1.60! Einstein's has grown by but half a penny. Euclid perfects his victory dance.

Year Two. Euclid's 40% loss puts him at 96 cents. He's unconcerned; the next 60% profit's just around the corner. Einstein? But a penny to show for two years' effort.

You probably guess how it ends. Euclid continues to make huge 60% profits followed by apparently smaller 40% losses, but somehow keeps falling further behind! He cries foul. "Einstein tricked me into going first! I want the profitable year to come after the losing year. That way my big wins come after my smaller loss! Ha!" Einstein graciously agrees both to the rematch and Euclid's new rules.

Year One. Euclid now has only 60 cents but salivates at the coming 60% gain. Einstein, as before, is up by but half a penny.

Year Two. Einstein again has only one penny of profit to show for his two years. Euclid? By some horrible legerdemain he has exactly the same $0.96 he had the first time! The match continues but Euclid is smart enough to see it's already over. By Year Ten he now knows he'll have but 82 cents while Einstein has his dollar plus a nickel profit. The referee calls the match. Had it continued, Year 40 would have shown Euclid with 44 cents, Einstein $1.28.

Sorry Euclid, better luck next time. How can this be? How and why does Euclid's super powered money machine lose? He seemed to have such a great punch!

Einstein counsels Euclid. Volatility is his problem. Yes, the average of +60% and -40% is +10%. But the geometric or compound return of multiplying the profit on the loss (or vice-versa) is a negative: -4%. (The "Father of Geometry" is particularly chagrined to learn the term used for compounding is called a geometric return).

A famous quip is "If your head is in the freezer, and your feet in the fire, are you comfortable on average?" Einstein used a similar image to explain his Theory of Relativity: "A minute sitting on a hot stove may seem like an hour; an hour sitting on the couch with your girlfriend may seem like a minute."

For fun, the two genius mathematicians agree to another race. Euclid having learned his lesson (he thinks) asks if he can cut his volatility down by an impressive factor of ten: instead of up 60% and down 40% he wants up 6% down 4%. When offered the same tenfold increase Einstein says he wants only a factor of two: 1% each year instead of 0.5%.

Sure enough, Euclid does better. Enough to make a small profit every two years now instead of a loss. But amazingly he still cannot beat Einstein at even Einstein's one percent each year! Einstein explains: the volatility effect is so powerful that a consistent one percent beats an inconsistent 2% in this and many other scenarios.

So there you have it. Keep a lid on the volatility of returns. Otherwise you may get knocked out. Now you know why investors so prize consistency and so loathe volatility.

Difficult. Very difficult, but don't despair! Soon we will be introduced to another mathematical buddy who will be of great help.

# Something from Nothing

"Rumble in the Jungle" taught us (and Euclid!) many things...

- Volatility is bad.
- Average return is deceptive.
- Geometric or compound return is what matters.
- Sequence of returns doesn't matter.
- The compound effect of volatility is not linear.

There's a delightful little children's book adapted from a Jewish folktale called *"Something from Nothing"* in which a grandfather gives his grandson the gift of imagination, teaching him to use his mind.

A warm welcome for our next guest please! Say hello to Harry Markowitz.

We're on our feet. Once you appreciate what Harry has given us, you too may want to give him a standing ovation. Harry may look like a little old balding economist, and Harry may have become famous as an economist, but we think Harry really is an Alchemist. A Wizard. Why? Can he turn base metals into rare Earths? Does he spin straw into gold?

Nope.

Better.

Harry makes Something from Nothing. No assistant, no equipment, no props. Using but his mind.

And he wrote it all down! He showed us how to do it too!

The Nobel was the least we could do. Harry won for something called Modern Portfolio Theory. Looking it up one learns it's how much of the civilized world manages money today. As theories are, it's constantly challenged, improved and of course someday replaced. But we are here today to praise Harry not to bury him.

We call your attention to just a single attribute of MPT which strictly speaking Harry didn't even invent, he merely showed us the importance of using it properly. It's an elegant counter-intuitive answer to the volatility that wiped out our friend Euclid earlier. Harry showed us how a tool that hurts also can be a tool that helps.

Dim the lights, please. Let's watch Harry's gift at work.

We have here an investment which after six periods earns a net profit (geometric return) of 1%. Call it investment "A":

"A": +9.0%, -8.0%, +8.0%, -7.0%, +9.0% -8.0% = +1.0%

Next, a similar investment "B". After the same periods it earns the same net 1%:

"B": -8.0%, +8.0%, -7.0%, +9.0%, -8.0%, +9.0% = +1.0%

They look similar, almost identical. In fact (to show Harry's gift is all the more amazing) they even are identical. The only difference is the order of the returns (which, as Euclid learned earlier, doesn't affect the end result one iota).

Hard to get excited about one over the other. Wouldn't matter. That's what Alice (she likes "A") and Barney ("B") do. In the end, yes, each has the exact same 1%. Didn't matter.

But hold that thought. Quiet please. Spotlight. Harry's about to do his magic! Can he make something out of nothing? Can 1 + 1 be anything but two?

Charlie gives his money to Harry. Charlie's not as dumb as he looks. In fact he's read a little about MPT. Knows what Harry will do.

But exactly what can Harry do, anyway? Put half your money in "A" and half in "B" you get half of 1% plus half of 1%, which equals half of 2% (otherwise known as 1%). In other words, if you average 1% and 1% you get 1%.

Doesn't worry Harry. He puts half of Charlie's money in "A", half in "B". Now we wait. Harry touches nothing. Abracadabra.

Can he average 1 and 1 to get something larger than one? Like maybe two?

Time's up.

Out pops Charlie's profit of...we hold our breath... two...two...please...two... and...it's... THREE!

Wait, what?

How on Earth did Harry do this? Half of one plus half of one makes three?

Recall we said Harry not only makes something from nothing, he wrote it down so we can too!

Here's what he did. He did... nothing.

Absolutely nothing. Used his mind to realize the same effect that hurt Euclid can be harnessed in reverse. High volatility hurts. Shouldn't low volatility help?

Charlie's investment:

"C": +0.5%, +0.0%, +0.5%, +1.0%, +0.5%, +0.5% = +3.0%

The secret is the "r" word ("r" in statistics is correlation). We don't want it. We want UN-correlated returns. "A" and "B" are nicely uncorrelated. Their volatilities tend to cancel out, giving Charlie the smooth opposite of "A" or "B".

If only Euclid had met Harry! He'd combine his same +60% -40% with a similar uncorrelated one. Would have blown Einstein away. Yeah, yeah. Coulda woulda shoulda.

For us, the lesson's clear. Volatility still is not our friend, but we don't have to shun it. We can harness it. Yolk it to other, similar (but uncorrelated) volatility and have the best of both worlds. This is what those of us who see the power of Harry's gift seek.

It's not easy.

In fact it's devilishly difficult. Just one obstacle is it's hard to know—in advance—what correlations will be in the future.

Nevertheless, safe to say that two different investments usually will be, well, different.

Any difference at all is something less than perfect correlation and thus an opportunity for us to enjoy the benefit of uncorrelated diversification. Something from Nothing.

This has been called "the only free lunch in investing."

Harry is picking up the check. Delicious. Thank you, Harry!

18

# Of Torture and the S&P 500

An MIT graduate student in Finance back-tests the heck out of data. Hundreds of markets, thousands of variables, millions of instruments, billions of scenarios, quadrillions of combinations (maybe more, he's no longer sure).

The computer grinds through the combinations. Exhaustive enumeration. Brute force. It labors quietly, effortlessly, without rest.

Not so our grad student. His dissertation chair says unless he finds new discoveries he can forget about that Ph.D. Oh, and be sure the discoveries are extraordinarily profitable ones, too (the professor has bills to pay).

In very short supply are our grad student's needs: food, sleep, praise, bathing, sex. So far his only discovery is the correlation between those last two needs. He approaches nervous breakdown. His unsympathetic professor knows there's lots more where he came from.

Our grad student tells the computer to torture the data more aggressively. If water-boarding the S&P 500 won't make it talk, perhaps electrodes under the fingernails? On the genitals? The answers are there. He knows that it knows. He will make it talk.

Gradually the hapless victim spills the beans.

Data always will confess if tortured. Always.

Presto! He finds 84 inputs with significant correlation to the movement of IBM stock price. 76 variables for Microsoft. 112 for Amazon. He works now with renewed energy. The exhausted S&P sings like a bird. The correlations are amazing. This will produce wealth beyond Croesus. Eureka. Eureka!

Everyone's happy. All's well that ends well. Our boy gets not only his PhD. but co-authorship of the journal article with his professor (already planning his Martha's Vineyard compound).

Only the battered S&P 500—slinking away to heal its wounds—is unimpressed.

Oops. Would that it were so simple. Sorry, Mr. MIT. Wrong. So Wrong.

The concept of curve-fitting is happening. When we curve-fit we carefully and selectively find and take into account all sorts of variables that are correlated, and just as carefully exclude all sorts of variables that are not correlated.

What's wrong with that? Isn't the whole idea to discover what is and is not correlated?

Yes, but we have a tense problem here. Are we sure we're discovering things that "are" correlated, not just "were" correlated? Is there a causality or are we just being "human" again and projecting it onto the data?

More importantly, even "are" correlated isn't profitable. What we need is "will be" correlated! The investment road is littered with the bodies of correlations that did not persist into the future.

There's no way to completely avoid curve-fitting. There are ways to reduce it. There are ways to attempt to purge it after the fact. A variety of statistical techniques.

Also the basic "smell test": is there a plausible explanation for "why" a causal relationship "should" exist?

Uh oh. Did we wring a confession from an innocent suspect?

The S&P, in a safe house, through its attorney, says nothing.

# Is the Water Too High,
# or Are We Too Short ?

Our sources (with our ear to the train track rails) are telling us something financially frightening. If we leave our head indefinitely here on the rails it will be physically frightening as well, so let us stand up and explain. This is what's happening...and when it does what we believe naturally comes in the months following.

"Insurance" sales are prevalent on Wall Street. They take several forms and are fundamental to one of financial markets' vital roles: those with appetite for risk— and (presumed) ability to accept it—assume it from those who find it dangerous or undesirable.

They are compensated for doing so. Common examples include commodity futures allowing a farmer to plant a crop contracting in advance for the sale price, equity index "put" options hedging a stock portfolio against crashes, etc.

Usually the provider of insurance is compensated adequately and on average makes money. "Usually" however is very much not the same as "always". Sometimes it just happens that the house loses.

What does this have to do with hedge funds? Glad you asked.

Typically, certain hedge fund strategies are short volatility. Usually the "vig" is in their favor, but sometimes stuff happens. Sometimes tremendous volatility... and the correlations between the stocks begin rising. Tune in to financial channels for dozens of confident—and conflicting—expert opinions on the cause: China, interest rates, energy, whatever. (We have no clue) is causing increased volatility. In fact, the mere fact that the hedge funds are short volatility may be causing the problem (a fascinating story in itself, which we will explore another time).

For now, just be aware that bad things begin happening to many hedge funds. Very bad things indeed. Extremely bad. A gentleman at one of our prime brokers delicately described it as "getting their heads ripped off". They are short volatility. Not only are they losing money, but they are forced to re-balance their portfolios in a desperate—continuing, escalating, and expensive—effort to try to stay above water. Unfortunately, they can't swim—not against a tsunami. Here is how the game works... or doesn't.

A hedge fund sells volatility. Doesn't matter whether it's implicit or explicit—it's still volatility. Volatility—implied or realized—jumps. Doesn't matter why. Oopsie. Hedge fund loses money. A lot of money. Too much money. Too fast. In what seems the blink of an eye, hedge fund is down over 30%. Here is where the fun starts. You may be hearing horror stories.

A hedge fund faced with big loses has a problem. Actually several problems. Not simply the losses. Not even the withdrawals. The profit sharing compensation scheme (usually about 20% of profits) is in jeopardy. They have to get back to their "high water mark" and recover that 30%+ before they can again participate. In fact they have to make back approaching 50% now (that darn geometric compounding thing again!) to get back noticeably above water level.

What to do? Oh, I have an idea! Let's close the fund. Give everyone what money they have left. Open a brand new fund, telling investors we have learned from our mistakes and are very, very, very likely to outperform as a result. After all, how could we have lost so much and not learned something, right? As well, that unreachable high water mark vanishes, and we get a "do over".

Sounds odd and unfair to investors? Yet not completely unreasonable. It is sometimes said (and very true) both that "good judgment is the result of experience" and also that "experience is the result of bad judgment." Unamusing as it may be to investors suffering through the painful educational events unfolding, managers who live to fight another day are unlikely to make the same mistake again.

So there you have it. Listen, with an ear to the rails and you may hear the sound of a disaster story (or many).

If the water (mark) seems too high it is only because hedge funds are too short (volatility).

# "A Penny for Your Thoughts"

Ever wonder why when a company misses by just a penny that it gets clobbered? We have a theory... CFO's won't like it... But let's give this one a try...

Super Tech Widget had an order that canceled late in the quarter. They at this fine firm tend to be liberal with revenue recognition and kind of, or actually more appropriately had to, recognize that advanced revenue to make the quarter estimate of 55 cents...

What to do? Jeez, "We have to do something, this is terrible"...

They go to work... Not to "cook the books". Microwave them! "You know the land we own in Florida? Lets mark it up." "That severance package for the old CEO? Let's defer recognition until next year".

Any CFO worth his Golden Parachute has a locked "emergency drawer" full of contingencies... ways to Deep Fat Fry the books until a nice Golden brown... the color of the Golden Egg. Providing investors with assurance that the Golden Goose is still in there laying 'em. Cranking 'em out in fact.

Only those in the Executive Suite know whether in fact the Golden Goose really is still cranking 'em out. Or whether that big order cancellation really means their goose is cooked...

27

On and on, and around and around, it goes... Where she stops, only the CFO knows... Usually when the CFO reaches into the drawer for another magic trick and to his horror gropes only the empty back of the drawer.

Finally after an exhausting—legal? who knows?—search for earnings, they still fall a penny short... Good effort though! The embarrassment of falling short, but just a penny is not great, but way better than the 40 cents they would have had to report without Herculean efforts.

On the other hand we have their competitor, Super Duper Widget.

They actually captured that canceled order and got the business! Their estimate of 55 cents is going to be beaten. Easy. Should we do anything? Is the Pope Catholic? So what to do? While it would be nice to pound our chest and jump for joy, is that prudent? Next quarter will come, we have to beat... then the following quarter... Hmmm...

Everyone knows investors like consistency. Markets really like consistency. Analysts positively love consistency.

"That land we have in California... Let's mark it down. Let's move ahead the vesting schedule of our employees"...

I think you get the idea. Duper "manages" to go from a profit of 70 cents to a profit of 56 cents... Well done! They beat by a penny, the stock jumps a lot and they now have the firepower "in the drawer" to beat for the foreseeable future...

So you see, when somebody misses or beats by a penny, maybe the reality is being dampened by managing earnings. The reality is much more severe. That is why slight earning surprise can be so important...

Another name for this school of thought is the "Cockroach Theory".

So named because earnings disappointments are like cockroaches. If you walk to your refrigerator in the middle of the night and hear the sickening crunch of a cockroach under your foot, you know without even turning on the light that this is not the only one in your kitchen.

Earnings disappointments are like cockroaches in that "there's never only one."

Hoping the first earnings disappointment is the only one is highly similar to hoping the first cockroach is the only one. Both approaches have a similar expectation of success. Possible? Yes. Probable? Ha.

"But they only missed by a penny."

So.

"A penny for your thoughts?" Maybe a small fortune?

# How to Lose Money

Years ago we had the privilege to meet the chair of one of our venture investors, a very refined British gentleman named Ivan. After dinner, Ivan leaned in, lowered his voice and—in a scene to pale Dustin Hoffman's famous "Plastics" moment from "The Graduate"—gravely intoned, "My friend, I will share with you the secret of our success."

After an appropriately (agonizingly) long pause, he said very quietly, "We not only know how to make money. We also know how to lose money." After this he reclined back in his chair, a satisfied sigh, a smile, a puff on the obligatory cigar, and silence (presumably for us to contemplate in fullness this pearl of great price).

We have to admit we were disappointed. Thanking him solemnly, we tried not to show it but fear we displayed our ignorance. Later, the head of his local office (now a friend, investor with us, successful VC in his own right) explained. Wherever you are Ivan, we apologize! As we've aged—perhaps even matured—we include that evening's advice with the very best investing lessons we can count on one hand.

Permit us to be less cryptic than Ivan was.

The ability to stay with a loss when appropriate but not when inappropriate is extraordinarily valuable. As "The Gambler" put it, ya gotta know when to hold 'em, know when to fold 'em. But how? The Wall Street bromide "Cut your losses, let your winners ride?" Better than nothing, but Ivan can help us do better.

We like Will Rogers' famous advice on making money in stocks: "It's easy. You buy stocks. When they go up, you sell them". Uh… but if they don't go up? Our man Will covered that too. "Then don't buy them of course."

This isn't just a joke. One tries to buy stocks that go up. Or at least has "expectation" (a mathematical term in this context) of going up. Follow Will's advice and we're on our way to follow Ivan's. Perhaps the biggest difference between gambling and investing is that word: expectation. In both, one contributes money hoping to receive more. Gambling is hoping to win despite a negative expectation. Investing is hoping to win because of a positive expectation.

This is valuable. But not Ivan's most valuable advice, not by a long shot.

We must know that losing money is inevitable. We must expect it. Must—and this is a biggie—know how much money to lose is reasonable. Even more important of course is knowing how much is unreasonable (a topic unto itself, to which we will return in future). In other words, one has to "know how" to lose money.

But wait, there's more.

To us the most valuable part has been psychological. One has to know how to fight the urge to panic. To "Do something!" when the fecal material is hitting the fan. We like to say, "A system is not for when it's working. A system is for when it's not working." Dad loved Kipling. Two lines from the famous poem "If" apply:

> *"If you can keep your head when all about you…*
> *Are losing theirs and blaming it on you…"*

This doesn't mean just watch with Zen-like calm while money hemorrhages from the account.

It does mean seek the Zen-like calm while knowing what losses—under what measurable circumstances—are mathematically expected, and therefore by definition tolerable.

Outside of that is by definition not tolerable.

Now, we are using Ivan's advice.

Now, we also know how to lose money.

# "Story" Stocks

What separates a "True Story" from a "Fairy Tale"?

How can we know what is potentially real and what simply a representation to convince us of something that may never happen?

SuperTech Widget wants to do an initial public offering (IPO). Super is heavily owned by venture capital firms and insiders. Super has a Story. They've done a super job of technology or marketing or something. Could be huge and profitable.

That's still yet to be known. What's not yet to be known however, is that Super wants cash—lots of it. Also, for the owners, it's Time to Cash In...

They go to the Wall Street Bankers for "advice". All the big firms know they're in competition (the "Beauty Contest"). They need to convince Super to use them as banker for the IPO. If you are one of those bankers, you'd better have your industry analyst recommend the stock. In fact "Pound the Table" with conviction.

Analyst reports on SuperTech begin to show an upswing. Bank A wins the deal as lead manager. Banks B and C get "place" and "show" positions as co-managers. Banks D, E and F are shut out for now. But every banker wants what comes next... additional financing roles—debt or equity—that SuperTech Widget will need to do in a year to stay afloat.

Thus every analyst from every firm is subtly—or maybe not subtly—encouraged to recommend the stock so they appeal to the company for the next Beauty Contest. It is easy to understand the conflict of interest here, between analysts and investors.

Broker ratings range from "Strong Buy" to "Buy", "Hold", "Sell" and "Strong Sell". You'd expect them roughly equally split buys and sells. You'd be wrong.

Last week, a very typical one, in our database of 5000+ stocks, what percentage would you guess are Strong Buy? Strong Sell? The answers are 51% and 3%. It's Lake Wobegone: all the children are above-average.

So back to our question: how to know? How to differentiate a good "Story" from a "Fairy Tale"?

Examine evidence and remove emotion from the process. Believe in nothing, seek facts and verify them. Facts are all around us. Here's a few...

Momentum. If the stock is languishing or going lower in spite of bullish analyst recommendations, beware.

Earnings. Profit. This is the "Show Me The Money!" method. Positive earnings surprises too are key. If a company actually produces results the Story becomes verified. If not, a Fairy Tale may be in the making.

What are hedge funds doing? Would you rather bet on aggressive thinkers with only profit in mind or analysts who may have profit from the next deal in mind?

Similarly Insiders. Watch not what they say but what they do. They have a pretty good clue. We like to say, "I don't have to know. I just have to know who knows."

Mathematical formulas and measures of value (price-to-earnings, price-to-sales, etc.) are unable to lunch with or be schmoozed by an analyst.

One of our favorite sayings—with which we've frightened away more than one potential investor—is, "I don't know what I own. But I know why I own it." A lighthearted description of a very serious process. Fundamental, actually. Why we invest is more important that in what we invest. Be far more concerned with the characteristics of the positions than the "story" of the individual companies.

If we are less concerned with the stories in the portfolio, does this imply picking stocks "top down" using "themes"? Actually, no. Pick stocks one at a time, bottom-up, but seek verifiable facts rather than listening to appealing stories. In fact, Stories can include fantasies.

"Stories", like "ideas" and "sure things" belong in your experience base. They are things to note and ways teach ourselves. They should be part of our process, not our portfolio.

# Mean Reversion... or
# Mean Perversion ?

Mean reversion is a concept well studied in statistics but often falsely applied. A well known study observed that children of tall adults tend to be slightly shorter than their parents. The concept applies to many things: when something gets "extreme" it is more likely to get back to "normal"...

Ok. Got it. But as usual, how to apply this to investing? Also as usual, the Devil is in the details. Where is it applicable? How far is extreme? When will it revert?

Examples abound. The famous "Gambler's Fallacy": the belief that if a coin has come up "heads" (or the roulette ball "black") many times in a row, the opposite now is "due". The bedrock of the palatial casinos of Vegas and Macau. The simple belief behind perhaps the largest sustained transfer of wealth in human history (from the mathematically challenged to the mathematically knowledgeable).

Our first home in the canyons of West Los Angeles was ruined by a flood. We fled for our lives, returning to floor-to-ceiling mud from the hills above. A city engineer soberly informed us it was a "100 year Rain" (expected only once every 100 years). Two years later the same thing. The same man—with straight face and no sense of irony whatsoever—informed us this, then, simply must have been a "500-year Rain"… Possible, we suppose. But unlikely.

More likely? The extremely poor grasp of basic statistics from which almost all of us suffer. All of us we suppose may be excused. Unfortunately however this ignorance extends to those charged with our financial and even physical safety. A depressingly long list, from those who regulate stock markets to those who plan for earthquakes. It comes as no surprise that those who suffer if wrong—insurance actuaries, professional options traders—make these mistakes far less than those who risk others' life or money—politicians, government agencies, TV reporters.

Let's try to understand how it works. Let's vastly oversimplify a complex branch of statistics. Maybe you've heard of the so-called "normal distribution" (aka the "bell curve") in which events at both extremes have very low probability. It's used to predict probability of countless events. Little known except to advanced statistics wonks is that the normal distribution isn't the only one. There are other curves. Of particular interest are those distributions with so-called "fat tails" where the rare events at the extremes occur just slightly more often than the normal distribution.

This is not a small thing. What if the probability of many events—events with small probabilities but huge impacts—was just a little bit higher? Would just a tiny difference in probability make much of a difference in real life? What if the largest stock market crashes and most destructive hurricanes were just a little bit more likely than we think? An excellent book on the subject, *The Black Swan* by Nassim Taleb explains it well and its author made himself wealthy acting on its principles.

It gets worse.

Even if we resist our Humanity and correctly get on the right side of probability, there's the little matter of timing.

Early in our career we realized we were a pretty good judge not of good stocks but of bad ones. We correctly saw business after business which we didn't like and sure enough, eventually many of them cratered. Often we shorted the stocks. We'd be patting ourselves on the back here but for a little problem. We lost money.

We correctly identified the future but direction wasn't enough. Often these "story stocks" of these lousy businesses kept going up for awhile after we identified them. Sometimes quite awhile. More than occasionally, long enough to inflict enough losses that we had to give up. As Lord Keynes is said to have quipped, "The Market can remain Irrational longer than You can remain Solvent."

Timing is everything.

After thousands of observations of the Red Sox we find they are actually slightly MORE likely to win the next game than the betting odds suggest. Don't quit your day job on this information; bookies have to make money too.

How about the reverse, the so-called "hot hand"? We go now go to the Philly Sixers season 1980, 1981. Sorry, gentlemen on the bench. Only one player had the slightest momentum on shots, Julius Erving. With one other player who had no correlation to the previous shot, all others were LESS likely to follow a good shot with a good shot. We believe in mean reversion when it does not exist. We believe in momentum when it does not exist.

The moral of this story is (once again) stop trusting your Human perception. Learn mathematics. Act on mathematics.

# All Aboard !

Have you ever given a thought to what a train engineer really can do? We speak of the engineer "driving" the train but that's really kind of a funny misnomer. All he or she can do is go faster or slower. Or they can stop. Those are the substantive options. That's about it. Someone up the tracks decides whether that train goes to Albany or Buffalo. Not our engineer.

We guess the engineer also can simply jump out of the train and leave it to someone else, but that is a bit of a mess for the engineer, isn't it? Frankly, as a passenger, that's also a bit worrisome.

Our point? Investing is the same.

We can go faster or slower (increase or decrease our investment, increase or decrease leverage). We can stop the train (get out, close out the position). Or we can jump ship (quit, get fired, let someone else deal with it or clean up the mess).

Not many options, especially after the train's left the station.

So what does this have to do with anything?

It simply means that those who work so hard to make earnings forecasts, predict stock prices, blah, blah, blah... either are pretending that they are unaware that they cannot steer the train, or (worse) have no idea that they cannot steer the train.

The most rational response to this knowledge should be profoundly relaxing. An officer of the company (the gal or guy "up the line") will decide whether the train (company) heads to Albany or Buffalo, and make the appropriate changes to the switching apparatus well before our engineer rolls over it (regardless of whether going fast or slow).

We on the train, hopefully were not planning to go to Chicago.

Who knows? Who can know? No one...

Those who trade options, table top, strangles, straddles, etc., have an assumption that they can steer the train (we will go into that some other time). For now however, we must realize that we actually have no idea where the train is going.

We may however know the train went to Albany 55% of the time, Buffalo 45% of the time.

Chicago? Oopsie. That actually would be a bit of a concern.

We wind up at the wrong place—not according to the train schedule—a lot. That is not at all the concern. In fact it would be irrational to concern ourselves or waste resources trying. Irrationality however—as we mention often—is Human beings' middle name, or at least seems especially so in the world of investing.

We should concern ourselves only with what may help us divine the destination toward which we are hurtling down the track.

We should concern ourselves with probabilities.

With trying to read any "tea leaves" that might give us an indication of what "the guy up the tracks" is thinking and doing (eg., short interest, insider trader actions).

We should not delude ourselves into thinking we have any control over where the train is going. We should not even think we have much (if any) knowledge of where the train is going.

We do think we should be able to divine a small bit of useful knowledge about where the guys up the track may be ordering the engineer to go.

Enjoy your trip.

We hope you arrive at your intended destination.

# Learning by Doing

Research shows one of the strongest, most effective ways to create lasting memory is through experience. Physical action burns information into memory stronger than reading about it or being instructed. We all know this from experience anyway. Nothing quite like touching a live electrical wire to cement the memory.

For obvious reasons this method has its downsides. In investing as in electricity. Losing pots of money is a less than ideal learning tool. But extremely effective.

Losses, of course, are inevitable. Learning from mistakes is not. Why was it made? What is generalizable? How best not to do it again? How best not to forget?

Long ago (1970s!) as a grad student we earned the princely sum of $1,200 for a Summer's hard union labor in a sweltering warehouse. We and our earnings walked into a brokerage and said, "fleece me." (I think we said invest, but the "financial consultant" easily grasped the situation). She found a new issue coming out the very next day! No waiting! 100 shares. $12. The exact amount we had!

That evening, sharing our maiden voyage with veteran trader Uncle Mike, he asked how we got a piece of a new issue (usually reserved for a firm's best clients). We assured him it was because we had impressed the broker with our intelligence.

We think some of that long-bankrupt company's directors may yet still be in jail.

Next we'll talk about one way to avoid repeating this mistake.

# "Where I'll See It"

Decades ago, visiting the office of a venture investor in our software firm, we noticed on a wall facing his desk a very elaborately, prominently framed document. Walking over to take a closer look, we saw a stock certificate for several hundred thousand shares of Equity Funding Corporation.

The name rang no bells and we assumed yet another trophy of this brilliant, taciturn man. Yet placement in the office was such that the visitor might or might not even notice it. He, on the other hand, almost could not possibly avoid seeing it. We asked about it.

"Look it up", he chuckled. We found one of the largest securities crimes ever perpetrated. "Computer fraud," this backer of dozens of hugely successful software ventures later told us. "I keep it where I'm very sure I continue to see it."

Today, framed, in our office, is a stock certificate in our name for (a smaller amount of) the ZZZZ Best Co., Inc. Where we are sure we cannot fail to see it. If the name rings no bells for you, look it up.

Good judgment is the result of experience.

Experience is the result of bad judgment.

Old men enjoy giving good advice. Perhaps to console ourselves for no longer being able to serve as bad examples?

# The Other Side

Consider the "other guy". Perhaps the most basic part of any trade is at least two parties. For a transaction to occur there must be both willing buyer and seller.

Equally obvious, less often considered, is both buyer and seller, at the same instant, have opposite opinions of the asset's value. Seller's willing to get rid of the stock at this price. Buyer thinks it's a good price to buy. Each believes so strongly they even willingly pay more or get less (with transaction costs) than the agreed price.

Fascinating. All over the planet. All the time. The biggest electronic video game in the world. At any instant millions of people with more than opposite analysis.

Be always mindful we don't trade with "the market". The other side always is a person. For their own account or others. Even computer systems merely follow instruction from programmers (people) about how to determine value.

For 40+ years artificial intelligence ("AI") has been just on the verge of making humans obsolete in many venues. Of course eventually it will do so. Perhaps then the important societal functions of markets will be automated and the likes of us will have to learn other skills. For now however, we still trade with people or their electronic agents. For now knowledge of human cognitive behavior still is critical.

Never forget, the unseen participants in the game are people. As the father of value investing Ben Graham observed approaching a century ago, "The stock market is not a weighing machine. It is a voting machine."

# How about a game of "Jeopardy!"

Watson, the now-famous IBM "thinking" computer (named less for Sherlock Holmes' loyal partner in detection Doctor Watson than the founder of the IBM Corporation Thomas J. Watson) first won at chess in 1997 with a victory over Garry Kasparov, the reigning champion. More recently we know Watson as the computer which bested the reigning human champion in another venue, the popular game show "Jeopardy!"

In any case, it is now time to play "Jeopardy!" All players must wait until the host Alex Trebek reads all of each clue, after which a light is lit as a "ready" signal, then the first to activate their buzzer wins the first try to answer the question.

Watson's superior bank of facts was a known advantage. Less obvious beforehand, but painfully obvious as soon as the match began, was his superior ability to react. The human champions were known not just for encyclopedic knowledge but also their almost perfect timing: not so quickly as to "jump the gun" but virtually instantly when permitted. The ten milliseconds Watson needed to respond however, clearly was outside the range of mortal men.

There were many other examples. Watson not only knew the information better, he knew how much to bet. Those familiar with the concept saw that he knew what is called "optimal f" (the best amount to wager).

Ken Jennings, the bested champion, graciously and humorously wrote on his answer tablet, "I for one welcome the new computer overlords."

What does this all mean for us and investing?

First, the distinction between an immensely powerful tool and a self-aware one.

Machines that perform computation, information-retrieval, and even complex decision-making—as Watson demonstrated with his "Jeopardy!" win—are here. Powerful tools. They will have to pry them from our cold, dead fingers.

Conscious, self-aware machines are coming too, but not quite so quickly. The staple of science fiction—sentient machines take over the world and rapidly dispose of us inefficient humans—isn't likely anytime soon. Computers still trail two-year-olds at many tasks.

When Watson goes to Wall Street (he's probably there already) he confronts a challenge far greater than natural language: human emotion and irrationality. Make the goal narrow ("find the best spread for January's carry") and we merely have an intelligent articulate calculator assistant. Make the goal broad ("Go make as much money as you can") and our new mechanical surrogates (deep inside following human programming plus observed human experience and "wisdom") react to each other as we humans do today, but immeasurably faster... A bunch of hyper-manic super-humans. Imagine a huge stock market crash and recovery, each a few seconds long, several times a day). Unnerving. But nothing new.

Time for another ad-nauseum warnings about being too Human. We always think we're witnessing something new. Michael Lewis' well-written "Flash Boys" decried the unfair advantage some traders achieved by building super-fast paths to the trading floor, learning information precious milliseconds sooner. Hardly different from generations past who sought financial or political gain learning information sooner by telegraph or before that by carrier pigeon, or horseback rider. Fortunes have turned on less. Technology marches on. There is nothing new under the Sun. Tools get better and better. We must try to learn how to use them.

Farther away—but inevitable—are truly conscious self-aware machines with whom (if we are lucky) we will share our world. In Stanley Kubrick's classic "2001: A Space Odyssey" pilot asks computer, "Open the pod bay doors please Hal." There is no reply. He repeats. Hal (who decided the ship's mission is compromised by its humans) says, "I'm sorry Dave, I'm afraid I can't do that."

What will we do when our computer partner fails to do what we want it to do? Will we even know?

Beyond Kubrick's mutiny, there's also just plain old stupidity. Anyone who's written and debugged a computer program—or even wrestled with a recalcitrant search query—is familiar with the difference between "what I want you to do" and "what I told you to do."

This will occur evolutionarily. Already only masochists do complex or repetitive calculations by hand. Those of us who trade financial markets with algorithms will see our computers taken only from our cold dead hands.

At least until Watson quits to become founding partner of his own hedge fund.

# "A horse ! A horse ! My kingdom for a horse !"

"A horse! a horse! my kingdom for a horse!"

One of Shakespeare's best known lines. From the Bard's Richard III. 1594.

It is relevant we think, to a successful approach to investing.

The fuller text is this:

> *CATESBY:*
> *Rescue, my Lord of Norfolk, rescue, rescue!*
> *The king enacts more wonders thane a man.*
> *Daring an opposite to every danger.*
> *His horse is slain, and on foot he fights.*
> *Seeking for Richmond in the throat of death.*
> *Rescue my lord, or else the day is lost!*
>
> *KING RICHARD III:*
> *A horse! a horse! my kingdom for a horse!*
>
> *CATESBY:*
> *Withdraw my lord. I'll help you to a horse.*

Realize you are in battle.

Leaving out the beneficial effect of trade—I'm barefoot with more carrots than I can eat; you're hungry with too many shoes you've made—financial market transactions are trying to make money from our superior opinion of the value of an asset.

We've just noted that on the other side of each of our transactions is a party with essentially the opposite view of our own regarding the value of the asset being traded.

By definition both of us cannot be right. By definition the asset will go up or down, showing which one of us it is. It is financial war. Keeping score is easy. Extremely straightforward. Some call it profit or loss. Others simply call it money.

It's easy to get rattled in "the fog of war" but let's learn from history. Strategy and tactics, guts and heart, are important. Necessary in fact.

Necessary, but not sufficient.

History teaches that technology is even more important.

Throughout history, superior technology repeatedly and profoundly transforms battle. Examples so easy to think of... gunpowder, armor, cavalry, all manner of ground, naval and air craft. Check out Jared Diamond's excellent *"Guns, Germs and Steel"*. Show up for battle... learn your opponent has a devastating new paradigm shift and you don't? Bad, bad news for you.

For a long and important span of human history one of those technologies was the horse—permitting small numbers of cavalry to decimate larger numbers of foot soldiers.

The imagery is not inappropriate today.

Years ago traders with superior technology (faster couriers, telegraph, slide-rule or abacus, probability tables) had a big advantage. The technologies change but the idea's still exactly the same.

We must constantly try to improve our tools. Constantly be on the lookout for better ones. Constantly seeking the powerful leading edge where battles are won. Constantly avoiding the bleeding edge where battles are lost to unreliability or not-ready-for-Prime-Time.

The takeaway? If we aspire to be superior investors we should know how to find and evaluate tools just as a general seeks to know how to evaluate the next generation helmet or fighter jet.

Recall our commentary about Watson playing "Jeopardy!" and the early predictions about Artificial Intelligence. Be aware the world changes.

And thankful you have a horse.

# A backwards "K"

Have you ever seen a backwards capital-letter "K"? Hint: on a baseball scorecard?

Backwards. What's up with that?

In baseball notation, a strikeout is recorded by the letter "K". When the strikeout is that particular flavor where batter doesn't swing and miss, but the pitch instead is called, Strike Three—"caught looking"—the notation is write the "K" backwards.

Struck out looking isn't an athletic failure of competitive strength or stamina, etc. Struck out looking is an error in perception. Or judgment. Or both.

Perception and judgment are at least as important as brute force ability to generate profitable trades. We like to think we don't get "caught looking" often. A helpful tool is Behavioral Economics, a field which attempts to understand and explain how we *Homo sapiens* operate in the real world of economic decision-making. All reminders of the "know thyself" investing dogma. Have we mentioned this before?

From an unknown successful investor...

Some people make things happen.
Some people watch things happen.
Some people say, "What happened?"

# "Substitutions will happen as they occur"

Substitutions.

They happen or don't happen. Should or should not happen.

But they occur...

Takes us back to the Yale Bowl. Our friend and former colleague, Jeff Biss, a very energetic and enthusiastic third team scout team player with 1.5 legs, wants to play... Yale Football it is... Here it goes....

It is the fourth quarter of "The Game" 1986...

Jeff has been practicing all year, is sick to death of the bench and wants to play... As he has done throughout the year, he goes to his coach and asks, "Coach. I'm ready to play. When do I get to go in?"

Coach replies, in a soft Southern voice. He always addressed his players in the surname...

"Mr. Biss, What did you ask?"

"Coach, I just was asking when I could go in."

"What?" he replies, "When are you going to play?"

"Yes, coach. When?"

"Mr. Biss. Substitutions will happen as they occur."

Coach turns away to other matters. The subject, it seems, is closed.

Substitutions will happen as they occur? Really? What the heck is that?

So Jeff wanders around in a circle... wondering... What the heck...?

And there you have it...

Substitutions will happen as they occur.

"The Market" may or may not "discover" your brilliant analysis. Whether it will or will not? ...is unknown. If your analysis is solid, Mr. Market will reward your insight more often than he punishes your naivete.

What is not unknown however, is that Mr. Market operates on his own time. Not ours. He will not be rushed just because we are ready to play. He cannot be rushed. Our desires are not his concern. He has a game to play. He turns to other matters.

We can put ourselves in the game before Coach calls us. (After all, we are the team owner!) We can get in the game when we're losing badly, giving in to the very human urge to do <expletive deleted> something! (Yet another opportunity to fight to resist our Humanity). We can trade more frequently than planned. We can day-trade. It's our money.

Better to stick with the game plan. If the plan is good you stick with it. (If you're not sure, you shouldn't be trading it yet). If the plan is good. believe in that plan, and most of all, yourself.

"We're gonna dance with who brung us" was made famous by legendary Texas football coach Darrell Royal. The down-home homily with its fractured grammar has been quoted as often as any in football and in a wide variety of contexts far beyond sports. Well it should. Forget who brought you to the dance and you likely go home alone.

Hone your methods, attitudes and procedures. They are delightful when they make money, hopefully most of the time. They are a comfort when they don't make money. As we like to say, "A system is not for when it's working. A system is for when it's not working." Take action, substitute names in the portfolio only as they naturally "occur" according to your plan.

"Substitutions happen as they occur..." What a genius!

# Celebrities and Stocks

Friends and family know that we hate the outsize influence of celebrities in our culture. We've become sufficiently obnoxious about it that our presence no longer is welcome at a variety of otherwise enjoyable entertainment gatherings.

Why do we regale you with this self-centered trivia?

Because yet another of the Behavioral Economics principles behind our investing philosophy has its roots in the same human characteristics which cause most of us to listen to celebrities.

Look up terms such as halo effect, anchoring, repetition. Concepts such as these and many others influence our perception of value and desirability. Our comfort with our decisions. And so much more.

The number of experiments that demonstrate beyond any doubt just how manipulable our decision-making apparatus is can be sobering at best—if not profoundly disheartening.

This story however isn't about social commentary. Let's focus on the applicability to investing.

People, even investment professionals—especially investment professionals—give lip service to the advantages of being a "contrarian" investor.

"Buy when there is blood in the streets" (attributed to British nobleman Baron Rothschild) is solid advice.

Unfortunately, it requires a different kind of blood—ice water might be best—in one's veins.

Most of us Humans follow a different pattern.

There's comfort in the crowd.

Evolutionarily—no small point in how our brains are wired—there is safety too in the crowd.

The gazelle on the Serengeti is less likely to be eaten in the herd than alone. Our buddy Caveman Joe might have avoided being Guest of Honor at lunch with a saber tooth tiger had he stayed with his hunting crew.

To the floor of the New York Stock Exchange.

Following the old buck at the head of the herd is considerably less useful than on the African plain.

To be successful, we need to be aware of our genetic programming.

Follow clothing trends if you wish. Follow celebrities if you must. But force yourself not to follow the financial herd.

How?

Remove your discretionary ability to be driven by fear, or greed. Remove your ability to instinctively stay with the comfort of the herd. Remove your ability to follow the comfort of the "leader", be they glittering celebrity or famous investment pundit.

Remove your discretion.

Develop a discipline.

# "This Time is Different"

It's 1998. Your annoying brother-in-law has been bragging for years now about the obscene amounts of easy money he's made buying tech stocks. The man's an idiot. But you can't help but notice your long-suffering wife eying their new car...

1999. CNBC daily explains the new era in stocks. Warren Buffet is losing money. A dinosaur. Warren <expletive deleted> Buffet!!! Your brother-in-law vacations on the French Riviera, parties with B-list celebrities. The kid who mows your lawn quits (he's day-trading full time now).

2000. Finally you can stand it no longer. You call your broker. She puts you into Netscape and AOL. Congratulates you on your acumen.

We don't need to fill in the rest of the story, do we?

Fast forward.

2007. Your sister and her husband both quit their day jobs to flip real estate. Despite their 2001 bankruptcy they buy easily, with zero percent down. No worries mate, Fannie and Freddie guarantee the loans. Besides, everybody knows real estate only goes up.

Ok, ok. You get the idea.

Our brains are perfectly wired by evolution to be the worst possible kind of investor. It takes a long time of watching others make money before we finally accept the risk and join them, at the top of the market, just in time to be slaughtered with the rest of the sheep. Afterward—swearing we'll never do that again—we shun risk when we should embrace it, and again it takes a long time watching others make money before we again take the plunge.

Let's also put to rest the idea that such stupidity is confined to the retail masses.

Professional investors are worse.

The phenomenon called "window dressing" refers to professional investors "dressing up" their portfolios just before the end of the quarter, buying whichever stocks best preformed recently. This is so they look smart when the fund reports its holdings.

Amazing how many funds hold only winners! All mistakes have been purged. They do not exist. They never existed.

The effect of this of course is to reinforce the "herd effect." Winning stocks go higher. Losing ones go lower.

Of course just like the tech stock bubble of 2000 and real estate bubble half a dozen years later, eventually the music stops, the bubble bursts, the punchbowl is empty, and we run out of stupid metaphors.

One of our favorite books is *"This Time is Different"* by Carmen Reinhart and Kenneth Rogoff, a tome suitable for body-building when you tire of reading. Its subtitle (*"800 Years of Financial Folly"*) says it all. The book is a compilation of dry statistics which—taken together—are nothing less than stunning.

Human beings have always been, and are highly likely to remain, astonishingly reliable herd animals.

There truly is nothing new under the Sun.

You probably won't be able to change your emotions, instincts, or (lack of) judgment, but you can teach your brain to supervise them.

# Wise Guy Squirrel's Coin Toss

Pretend we're a squirrel in New Hampshire. Late November, few nuts for the long winter… Cold, getting desperate. Finally, after a long and difficult search… just before Christmas… we may have gathered enough for the winter… Relief!

But uh oh, "Wise Guy Squirrel" shows up from NYC..."I see you've lots of nuts there. Good for you! Lets play a game." We—in our New Hampshire innocence—listen. "Want to do double or nothing?" What would we do with twice as many nuts? If we lose, we starve. We tell Wise Guy go back to NYC and leave us alone.

What did we just do? We made it roughly certain that we'll survive the winter. Have children that would have children. We already knew that as a squirrel—or Human—we're hard-wired to hate losing more than like winning. Period.

If Wise Guy approaches a random person on the street, offers a fair coin ("promise it's fair!") and says, "Tell you what. If Heads you give me $100. If Tails I give you $100" almost anyone says no. Ok, Ok. So Wise Guy says, "If heads you give me $100, if Tails I give you $120", Hmmm... Getting close? Not really, as defined by the experiments, still too stressful a psychological stretch...

When do we start to play? As it turns out, research shows that when winning ratio to losing ratio in a random game reaches 1.5 to 1 we generally start to play. Our risk-averse nature clouds our thought. "We can't handle the truth." We want to keep our nuts. This makes us the worst investors imaginable! Wise Guy offered a free lunch for us on the Streets of NYC, but we could not see it.

# Popularity Contest

Many years ago we played the craps tables in Vegas. Not—we hasten to add—from any expectation of winning. Such thinking in our opinion would disqualify us from serious consideration to manage even our own money, much less anyone else's. No, we played in order to engage in a bit of bush-league arbitrage.

With a friend we bought one of the many math-oriented books on casino gambling, found the "best" bet (where the house's edge is smallest) so we'd have expectation (there's that word again!) of the longest playing time before the money ran out. The goal was to be "comped" for our losses, have a cheap vacation.

Our thinking not only was correct, but with discipline and on average we received much more in freebies than we lost. We'd converted a negative expectation into a positive one. Absent from our calculations were the effect of too many fatty buffet meals, hours standing in smoke-filled rooms drinking alcohol, and an hourly net profit below the poverty line... but we nevertheless thought ourselves quite clever.

We did this for a few years, escalating our bets. Our families enjoyed the increasing quality of rooms, food, gifts. We, on the other hand, put in long hours at the tables, our careful bets unchanging and indistinguishable from automatons. Before we quit, those few weeks each year resembled a twisted dystopian traditional family where Dad—never seen—always was at work, albeit at the craps table.

Unexpected aspects of this little misadventure however taught us a few lessons useful in investing.

The "best" bet (at that time for major Vegas casino rules, limits, comp) was called "Take the Don't and Lay the Odds". If you've ever played or even watched a busy craps table, you quickly see it's a very social game, perhaps the most social in the casino. Ritual and benedictions more complicated than most churches are performed upon the dice before they are sent on their mission. Pleasure and pain are shared group experiences. Raucous cheers erupt as the shooter makes his point, rewarding most everyone at the table. Silence and low groans greet their losses, the stick men quickly raking in most everyone's money.

"Most" everyone's. Not all.

Several bets on the table are "against" the shooter ("with" the house). Two of these we bet consistently. We quickly learned this made us unpopular. When everyone else won, we lost.

More importantly, when they all lost, we won. Comment (at minimum) ensued.

At first we tried sharing our "secret" math so they too could partake. The reaction couldn't have been colder had we suggested ritual sacrifice. Next we joked. ("Hey, come on over to the Dark Side!"). That too quickly stopped as more than one beefy inebriate suggested our parents had never married.

That the "popular" bet had a lower mathematical expectation interested no one.

Evolutionarily we were back on the Serengeti. Wildebeest sticking together as the casino Lion serially ate one at a time alive. That others (us) conflicted actually made the decision to confirm by differentiating from "enemy" that much easier.

An analogy too applies to short-selling—equally unpopular and for similar reasons —whose practitioners provide valuable services (free, we might add) to the ordinary investor who'll never short a single share. Identifying poor management (not to mention fraud), providing liquidity, policing prices, etc. Confirmed by reputable academic study after reputable academic study. Actually benefits society.

But it bothers the herd.

Stocks down? Must be the shorts manipulating the market. Would that we could. Don't bother regulators, politicians or media with facts. Those who are voluntarily different must be evil.

Once again, confirm again: Humans, evolutionarily, are not good investors.

We must fight our nature.

Where there is high level of agreement and comfort, chances are there will be losses rather than gains. Small statistical edges arise where there is misunderstanding, where there is less participation (and competition) and where the actions of those smart enough to participate can be discerned.

# Deltas and Dreams

This is a bit complex, but please listen. This is as pure as it gets. Volatility is mean reverting. It can't help itself.

There are two groups: those that buy index options, and those that sell. Buyers make leveraged bets. Sellers have no market opinion. They simply sell at an implied volatility and hedge the risk with futures. In other words, they cover their reverse bet by hedging "delta" (the chance the option will finish "in the money").

We go now to the options pit. Chicago. Why Chicago? We don't know, maybe pork bellies or something, ask Carl Sandburg, but it's the epicenter of futures markets in this country, as is New York for equities. Let's consider two scenarios....

One is crazy high implied volatility. All Hell breaking loose. The chance a strike (at the money) option is to be in the money? 50/50? Who knows? Who can know? So the seller—Chicago guy or gal—hedges their Delta (stock risk) at 50% even if the stock rises. Things are so nuts they hesitate to hedge. Could go either way, big time, so they drag their feet, finger on the trigger, waiting, watching...

The other is very low implied volatility. The S&P future is "in the money" so it will likely be exercised, things are not bouncing around very much. So we hedge it heavy, assume things don't change and the likelihood of exercise is big.

How simple is this mean reversion thing? Low volatility, hedge heavy. High volatility, hedge light. How beautiful and pure. It *has* to mean revert. Can't help it!

# Old and Dirty

Old and dirty rarely is most desirable. People like fresh, young, modern. There are exceptions. Maybe a dusty vintage from the wine cellar? Buried doubloons? Mostly however, we like new and clean.

We think historical back-testing data is a funny exception. We like ours old and we like ours dirty. The old part makes sense. The older the data go back, the more we have to test.

But dirty?

Dirty data has dirt in it. Errors. Untruths. Who wants that? Vendors try hard to get dirt *out* of their data. "Clean" historical data has been diligently, repeatedly, accuracy-checked. All known errors corrected. Done properly, this is expensive. The vendors who do the best job of this demand (and get) vastly higher prices for clean historical data.

Why would we prefer dirty?

Because real life is messy. The information we receive day-to-day in the real world contains truth and untruth, which we must try to separate.

(This is not, by the way, the serious problem of distilling the occasional droplet of fact from the fire-hose of intentional misinformation, advertising, political manipulation, and just plain astonishing stupidity that passes for "information" in our society. That's a much bigger problem—frankly, above our pay grade—and not for today. No, today we confront only the more prosaic problem of errors in historical financial data-sets.)

We want a special kind of dirt.

Not any old dirt. Random or additional error due to sloppiness is not it (we make enough on our own already, thank you very much). No, a very special kind: the most accurate representation of actual decision information—errors and all—at whatever moment back in time we are trying to replicate now.

To know if your system would have made a profit in July of 1994 the best errors are the ones it would have had to deal with as "fact" at that July 1994 time.

What we want is a time machine.

Fortunately, we have one. Being old, structured and obsessive has several downsides (often for those around us; ask our lovely wife). One of the upsides is that years ago we began to carefully archive data downloads. As a result we are able to replicate what we would have thought was fact at regular intervals in time. Not simulate. Replicate. What the world thought was fact at that moment. Because we actually captured it at that moment. Errors, inconsistencies, ambiguities and all.

Unchanged.

There are hundreds of different kinds of confusing errors in real-time real-life data. A simple example is unknown math error (eg. P=70, E=10 but P/E=23). Another: to compute 10-year return a vendor eliminates companies without 10 years of data, eliminating the messy problem of how to deal with bankruptcies, mergers, acquisitions, etc. This latter by the way is a classic example of "survivorship bias"... data which consists only of "survivors" extant at the time the database was created. This is what we would have if we searched for the top (or the bottom, or for that matter just wanted to rank all stocks by) any variable over some time period. You can't have a value for x months if you don't exist for x months.

Survivorship error also just happens to strongly favor returns shown when testing long-only strategies (because the crash-and-burn entries are not in it). Long-only investors are well over 90% of all investors (and all customers for databases and stock-picking systems). But that couldn't possibly reduce the incentive for database vendors to remove that error from their product could it?

Vendors may try to resolve errors and biases in a variety of ways. Whether the fix is sloppy or very detailed research with the benefit of hindsight, neither forces us to deal with real ambiguity in real time as happens in the real world. If however we are forced to deal with the errors and resolve the inconsistencies as we find them, we are perhaps better able to get a little closer to how best to deal with the present in order to try to divine the future.

Algorithms that back-test profits on clean data often fail in the real world.

So get dirty.

Or at least get real.

# The Demons

Do you ever have Demons? You know the ones. The ones that dance on the pillow at night. When you're most worried. When all you so desperately want is the briefest respite of sleep.

Sometimes late at night? Sometimes early in the morning? Socially? Financially? We cannot help you Socially, but we've a feeling we can help you defeat that special evil breed, the Financial Demon. Both he (why is it usually a he?) and his nasty little friends (they never come alone, do they?).

The ones that dance. The ones that cackle. The ones that whisper. "You're in very big trouble. You do know that don't you?" The ones that shout. "It's over! The bank. The bills. Your house. Family. Life. Over!" Then the whisperer again, "It's starting. It's happening. There's nothing you can do. Nothing. Nothing..."

We have them too. We know them well. We've even given some of them names. The Cash one, the Relationship one, the Net Worth one, the Retirement one, the Kids one, and the Health one... They are almost transparent how they hide, yet so physically strong! Different colors, probably shades of green I suppose. We've seen them up close but we've never really seen one, although in the darkened bedroom we can physically feel their presence.

We all stress too much sometimes, when sleep is either yet to be started or finished. Like it or not, the Demons live in the bedroom. They wait. They do not sleep. Ever. They wait patiently for us. The pillow is their favorite playground. They torment us with all the firepower they have... and the Demons have a lot of firepower... everything we have. Everything we give them.

What to do? Several techniques. Trust us, we've had a lot of time to practice this.

First of all, facts. This is why we have a discipline. "A system is not for when it's working. A system is for when it's not working." Follow your disciplines and two things are near certain: there will be losses, and they will fall within expected ranges. Not comfortable, but expected.

You can try reasoning with Financial Demons but they're seldom quieted by facts. Besides, they like to mess with the facts. Ours have their own spreadsheets, charts. A PowerPoint presentation on the ceiling of our bedroom! Little creeps. Emotion, not logic, is their playground.

We love Dr. Seuss. Cleverly hidden inside his books for children are both life's problems:

> *"Oh this Mess is so Big, and so Deep, and so Tall,*
> *We cannot clean it up. There is no way at all."*

and solutions:

> *"You have Brains in your Head, You have Feet in your Shoes,*
> *You can Navigate. Anywhere that you Choose!"*

Another technique is the Mantra. Repeat to yourself over and over. "We've been here before, haven't we?" "It is just possible this may not actually be the end of the world after all." Repeat, "I've been here before. I'll be here again." Repeat.

Our favorite. Give it right back to them. Laugh. Shoot right back, "That's it?" "That all you got?", "Really?" "That's the best you can do?"

The only actual solution. Hold their little faces into the pillow. They will protest. They will squirm. Their vicious little buddies will whisper louder. Whisper right back. Tell them, "You're next".

Take those Financial Demons, bury their faces in the pillow, and tell them, one at a time, that they are dismissed. They "don't get it". They need to die. They need to die so that you may live. Their sole reason for existence is to torment us. Peaceful coexistence is not possible. It's us or them.

In a last ditch effort, the Money Demon may cry out piteously, "I was only trying to help all along!" Do not let him up. He is the worst of Demons. Stick them all face down in the pillow. Do not let go until the job is finished. Then hold their little faces tighter into the pillow. Tighter. Until you're very sure they stop squirming.

These stories have lots of "Demon Killers" in them. Arrows for your quiver. We hope you enjoy them. Most of all, we hope you can sleep better.

Here's to a good night's sleep!

# Social Value

Do hedge funds contribute to society? What about mutual funds? Stock markets?

Sure, good funds reward their investors with returns, but isn't this at the expense of others? Not to mention the brokers who—like the Vegas House—collect their "vigorish" no matter who wins.

Our three children—all with professional degrees in various fields—inform us they were awarded diplomas from their prestigious universities without once being exposed to the idea that capital markets are anything other than places where one may bet on the fortunes of Apple Computer or Starbucks, exactly as one bets on Dallas or Miami at the Vegas sports book. The majority of people in Western democracies no longer hear that stock is actual ownership of a company.

This is dangerous. People unaware that capital markets enable a Steve Jobs or a Howard Schultz to finance or grow the companies that make their iPhone or Mocha Frappuccino have no reason to know or care whether such markets exist.

So what?

For all of civilized history—a very long time—until just maybe a century or so ago, society consisted of two classes. The minority of "landed gentry", who lived on income from land and productive assets such as a business. The rest of us lived—and died—with income solely from labor.

Most of the world still lives that way today. No matter whether nominally democratic, socialistic or communistic, with the exception of the Western democracies most countries consist of a kleptocratic few who live extremely well and the rest a huge majority of peasants.

Profound inequality still exists even in Western democracies. This is deplorable and our politicians seem capable only of posturing...conservatives with little plan beyond vague references to free markets...liberals bent on replacing those markets with redistribution as in the 60's song lyric "Tax the rich / Feed the poor / Till there are / No rich no more."

The Zeitgeist is that income inequality is the result of capitalism, and that socialism or even communism is "fairer". History teaches otherwise. We need to increase the opportunity of working-class people to become leisure-class people. Capital markets allow ordinary people to participate in the profits company owners earn. Capital markets usually are the root and largest source of countries'—and their people's—productivity and prosperity.

One of the really big deals of recent time is the ability of the average person to get a piece of those assets through stock ownership. The almost immeasurable improvement in living standards—the lowest-paid worker in Western democracies lives life the richest king couldn't dream of little more than a century ago: indoor plumbing, electricity, air travel, such magic as a smartphone.

Capitalism didn't just make these, it enabled a working class person to own the means of production and for the first time in human history some of the working class began to become members of the leisure-class. Markets are crucial.

And traders? Do they contribute anything to the financial ecology? Previously we noted that traders in markets ultimately and always are people and—importantly—no trade occurs without both willing buyer and seller. Note the word both.

Those who risk their own or investors' capital make markets. Without the other side of a trade your share of ownership is unavailable when you want to buy it or impossible to dispose of when you need to sell.

Without markets and liquidity your slice of Google won't feed you.

As a society we are forgetting all this at our peril.

Take time from your pursuit of profit to help educate media, regulators, educators, government. Before the golden goose is slain.

# Southie

We have something surprising to tell you. Published in April of 1991 in the New England Journal of Medicine no less.

Left handed people have a shorter life span than right handed people. Not just a measurable statistical difference either. No, a significant difference. Really significant. Frightening!

Researchers, who studied the deaths of 1,000 Southern Californians reported that right-handers, on average, live to be 75 years old. Left-handers typically died at age 66. My goodness!

The researchers, Dr. Diane F. Halpern of California State University at San Bernardino and Dr. Stanley Coren of the University of British Columbia, were nothing short of stunned.

We can try to posit the cause. Something of more accidental deaths with scissors or whatever. Maybe a harder life living in a right-handed world. Or maybe something more subtle? A sort of genetic difference that predetermines a shorter life span?

Whatever. It is what it is.

So what does this have to do with financial management? Nothing? Everything?

We will go with everything. Here is why...

South Paws are not equipped to live in this right-handed World. We as Humans are not equipped to invest money. We've covered several examples thus far. We are effectively investing with our left hand because it is what comes naturally to us. We simply are not equipped.

Is it behavior? Are left-handers more emotional? Flippant? Are we all South Paws when it comes to investing? Emotional seekers (and finders) of Causation where actually we are seeing only Correlation? Trying to live in the (investing) world for which we are slightly wrongly equipped? With the same—significantly different—result?

Over the past few hundred years—rather short for we *Homo sapiens*—left-handedness was shunned. Whether working in a factory, cutting something with a knife, or (more importantly regarding investing) in school. Today in America this happens less if at all. We are naturally left-handed. Throw with left hand, kick with left foot. But we write with our right hand, because we are so old that in school we were forcibly re-oriented to hold the pencil with our right hand. In much of the world this still is the norm: in school left handedness was unacceptable, period.

We *Homo sapiens* can adapt well. Really well. That's why we are here.

The rate of left-handers was artificially pushed down during the Victorian period, thus those who died early, even today tended to be left handed. The number of left-handers grew dramatically during the 20th century. Is it simply because left handed confessions have been a gradual process that is now accepted? Of course a majority today are relatively younger. They did not exist earlier.

In less tolerant nations, left-handed people tend to be less than 5% of the population. In more tolerant ones the percentage rises to over 12%. Genetic? Ha.

More fun facts: anthropologists studying painting and food records (Caveman Joe's tools) suggest 33% (yes, 33%) of people were really lefties long ago.

In an experiment in France in 2002, a task given to college students found exactly the same distribution. When asked to throw a ball, 9% left-handed. When asked to write, 8% left-handed. When asked to paint a negative image while blowing through a tube, exactly 33% used their left hand. We are back to 400,000 years ago. Exactly the number. Wow.

You might ask, "What does this have to do with investing?"

The cause or the effect?

The data may be flawed. The correlation may exist without knowing causation. Who knows? Who can know? What we do know is that with markets, we do not have to know.

We simply have to know who knows.

"To the man with a hammer in his hand, all the world is a nail..."

Sure can throw a good sinker though...

# Identity Crisis

There are many religions in the world of investing. The biggest have largely opposing views. Fundamental vs. Technical. Growth vs. Value. Bottom-up. Top-down. Sit even briefly in the pews of each Mother Church and you could get the impression that ecumenicism is not possible. The catechism of Fundamental is almost diametrically opposite of Technical. The ritual of Growth investors is apostasy to Value's followers. The orthodoxy of dedicated Bottom-Up stock pickers is heresy in (and grounds for excommunication from) the Top-Down temple.

Yet all appear to make money! Testaments of those made rich by each faith's healers are found easily, conveniently available day and night from Bloomberg, CNBC, networks' Business Channels, hundreds of magazines, thousands of books.

Are they all lying? No. Followers of most all of the major investing orthodoxies do make money. In fact, the closer they hew to a consistent, disciplined execution of the dictates of their chosen congregation, the more likely they are to achieve their goal of profitable return on their capital. Yet the more disciplined, the more different. Still—we allege—they all make money? How is that possible?

The first explanation is time. By this we mostly mean holding period. Growth and momentum adherents have a short time frame. Profit generally requires short term attention and vigilance. Value and fundamental investors usually are in for the long pull (or at least until the market "recognizes" the unrecognized value). The second reason: discipline. Holding on when all emotion screams cut and run.

The nexus of the two explanations is the difficult "know thyself". Who are you? How strong is your faith? When tested (by loss) will you falter?

Now back to the question. How can both be right? Did we not learn earlier that every trade by definition has opposing opinions on each side? That after transaction costs trading is even a less than zero sum game?

Consider Intergalactic Widget Industries (IWIN) trading at $100. Morris ("Mo" to his friends) is a momentum investor. He watched IWIN fall from $125, believes it will fall further. He places a sell (short) order. At the same moment, on the other side of the world, Valentina ("Val" to her intimates) is a value investor who believes IWIN worth $150, has been waiting for it to hit $100. She buys.

A month later IWIN's up to $110. Mo still believes his analysis, is willing to give it another month or five more dollars. Val's not even tempted to take her quick profit; it's not her discipline. She too believes her analysis. She holds. Another month. IWIN drops to $90. Mo grabs his short term profit and is off to the next stock. Val is unconcerned. A year later she sells at her $150. Both our heroes are happy.

An alternative scenario. The second month, when IWIN hit $90, Val decides this loss is unacceptable, sells. Mo holds out for a bigger pop, the stock just keeps going up from here, he eventually capitulates a year later at the $150 for a big loss. Both our protagonists lose. In this simple scenario Mo and Val lost because they got confused who they were. The short term investor who holds on too long, either seeking too much profit or—more often—failing to face a loss, stubbornly hoping. The value investor who loses his or her nerve and becomes a short term trader.

Short term traders make money. Long term traders make money. Those who get confused lose money. Decide who you are. Don't forget who you are!

Value. Fundamentals. Long holding period. Patience.

Momentum. Growth. Trading. In and out.

They both work. But mostly in isolation. Difficult together. Very difficult.

You are married. Wonderful wife. Wonderful life. That is the ideal "Value Trade".

At the bar with buddies. My Goodness...what a hot chick! (A "Momentum Trade").

Our former partner wistfully holds out one arm, "On the one hand, ya got your Security...", then turns to hold out the other arm, "On the other hand, ya got your Variety...". He sighs. "No matter how you try to kid yourself, the more you have of one, the less you have of the other..."

There you have it. Growth and Value. Yin and Yang. Each indisputably has their attractions. But do not bring home the Momentum girl to your Value wife, nor present the Value wife to the Momentum girl. Ever.

Individuals sometimes try to have both value and momentum in their investment style. Individuals sometimes try to have both security and variety in their personal relationships. Both usually end badly.

Rather simple, no?

# Let's Make a Deal !

This lesson cost us dearly when we were running a trading desk in London. Personally, not business, but it was 1988 and we were so young and so sure we were just "too cool for school." We were wrong.

To learn the lesson let's tune in now to the iconic game show that began in the 1960's, "Lets Make a Deal!" The finale segment at the end of each show. The creator and host, Monty Hall, asks the contestant to choose. Will it be "Door Number One, Door Number Two, or Door Number Three?"

We pick door Number One. Looking for the car. Behind the other two doors wait a dozen kitchen appliances…the consolation prize… or…a goat…or a cow…or a rooster… to bleat, moo or crow. To mock our decision-making stupidity in front of Mr. and Mrs. America… Monty bellows out toward the audience with hearty bonhomie, "Wonderful! Good job! You have a chance for the car!"

Prize model "The Lovely Carol Merrill" swings open gigantic numbered Door Number Two to reveal... Sure enough, there's our friend Belle the cow, heavy cow-herding bell ringing impossibly while she eyes the proceedings with a look of utter (or would that be udder?) disdain. After all, she not only knows exactly where the car is, but this definitely is not her first rodeo...

Monty's booming voice jerks us from our reverie. Back to reality. Crunch time. "Do you want to change your choice? Or stick with Door Number One?"

Soundless voices fairly scream in our head. "Stick!" "Switch!" The unseen, unknown product of a millions years' evolution crowds our unconscious. Regret Aversion. Ownership Bias. Endowment Effect. Herding Behavior. Framing Bias.

Sweat. Studio lights. Must be a million degrees in here. Did we just soil ourselves? We go to commercial break. A hundred coaches scream advice at the top of their lungs. From the front row a man bellows, "They were all ⅓. But Two's gone now! Three's now ⅔! It's Three! You idiot! It's simple math! Three! THREE!"

Is it possible he's right?

Back on the air. We manage to croak out, "I... I...want to switch Monty..."

Instantly we regret. Yes, Door Number Three used to be ⅓ chance. Yes, Door Number Two now is gone. But no, that doesn't mean Door Number Three is ⅔ chance. We forgot about Door number One. With a sinking feeling we recalculate, and realize math cannot help us here.

Math cannot help, but logic and psychology might.

What do cows and long-retired game shows have to do with investing?

Monty has inside information (oh, that thing again).

Always, always, always switch to Door Number Three...

Why?

Insider information. "I don't have to know. I just have to know who knows."

It's a TV show. Monty and The Lovely Carol Merrill know what's behind each door. Their job is to produce entertainment, so the audience watches all the way to the final commercial. It's pretty unlikely we'll see the car until the end of the show.

If our Door contains the car, Monty selects the Door with the appliances to be shown. This makes the contestant's last choice all the more exciting: all (the car) or nothing (the cow). Similarly, if our Door is the cow, Monty asks The Lovely Carol Merrill to fling wide the Door with the appliances. Again an exciting all-or-nothing finish. If we've picked the Door with the appliances, Monty and Carol still keep the car until last. The audience first sees our good friend Belle.

Hard to abandon our original decision. Too many of the Human errors to enumerate here. The pain of abandoning our original choice if it turns out to have been wrong. The perception of odds at the outset. Our brain's quick decision-making apparatus (the entire subject of an excellent book, *"Thinking, Fast and Slow"* by Daniel Kahneman) that brought our species—alive, we might add—out of the Serengeti into the television studio.

We Humans have this thing called "ownership bias" we associate what we own with our persona. If we "buy" Door Number One we have narrowed the scope of our thinking process. Thought and ego. To change and be wrong, although optimal here, is more difficult to consider.

On Wall Street, go ahead and change and accept the possibility of being wrong. You might win a really nice car!

# Survivor

It never ceases to amaze that Wall Street and the financial media, with all the money and glamor attached to success, all the supposed intelligence and sophistication, is in so many ways so very fundamentally naïve. There is of course real talent and strong research, but many gaping, persistent blind spots. Let's return to one, "Survivorship Bias." A simple concept really. Let's look at examples. Then we can have fun with the implications.

A Wall Street analyst, after combing (and of course, torturing) data, discovers that if she simply bought every stock that hit a low price of $2.00 over the last 20 years... she would have become fabulously rich. Again—as with our story of Mr. MIT water-boarding the S&P500—Eureka! Perhaps not... but why? Seems a winner...

The problem is that many stocks that hit $2.00 per share went on to go lower until... they vanished entirely. By definition they cannot be in any 20-year database. Those that quietly—or not so quietly—marched from two dollars to zero dollars, never to be seen again, are simply gone. Those companies that survived however, and actually thrived, are still there, with shining glory. These have impressed the quantitative analyst. Those that died have disappeared. (This also is another flavor of "History is written by the winners").

We can have fun with this concept (and the unwary be fooled by it) in many places all over Wall Street. If you read endless mutual fund studies you will notice that a strangely high number outperform the benchmark averages. How can this be?

We said most mutual fund managers reliably under-perform passive indices. Were we wrong? Again at Lake Wobegone where all of the children are above-average?

The mutual funds that underperformed, like the $2.00 stock that marched to nothingness, are simply gone. The sponsors closed the fund, fired the manager—who by the way moved on, ran another fund, through luck or skill finally managed to beat the indices for the first time in years and yes, is publishing only the new record—and the sub-par performance from before, no longer exists. A bit like Orwell's *1984*. It does not exist. It never existed. Thinking about it is a state crime.

The problem however is not limited to Wall Street. It occurs regularly in scientific research, government statistics (perhaps especially government statistics) and, well, you name it. Statistics are compiled and edited by people. History is written by the winners. Caveat emptor.

One of the strongest and most widespread fantasies in stock investing is the initial public offering. What equity investor hasn't daydreamed about having gotten a piece of a mega-success such as the IPO for Apple or Google? Who wouldn't love to "get in on the ground floor" of the next one and ride the elevator to the top?

Actual statistics however tell quite another story. We've not noticed it recently but for many decades *Forbes* magazine used to run a little article every few years showing what your return would have been had you received an allocation of every IPO for the last few years. In each and every case the results were astonishing. In each case, despite getting in on *all* the blockbusters, you would have turned a dollar into only a few pennies—generally between ten and twenty pennies. The reason we believe otherwise? Part of it is our Human nature again, remembering the fabulous successes we missed (which, like the winners of the war, are here to remind us of their success). But a bigger part is Survivorship Bias. The IPOs of companies that struggle and fail or are acquired at pennies on the dollar no longer exist in our mental database.

So what to do? Passive indices? Hide it in the mattress? A quick all-or-nothing trip to Vegas... put it all on Red?

As in all else in life... research, knowledge, homework. "Investigate before you invest". So tiresome. So true. Metrics of the best mutual fund managers, best ETFs, best hedge fund managers, best investment advisers, best investment publications, all are not difficult to find but neither are they advertised heavily. Spend as much time investigating where you put your money as you spend investigating a home or car (we certainly hope you do that too!) and you are likely to avoid many of the potholes in the road.

Simply being aware, to look for Survivorship Bias, is a big advantage.

# Encore

One of our most valuable concepts we embody in one of our favorite expressions: "Ideas go always into the procedure, never into the portfolio". By this we mean there is one very important characteristic of long term success as an investor that is *in addition* to all of the traditional characteristics such as profit, discipline, etc. What is that characteristic? Repeatability.

It's not enough to make decisions which make money. It's important to make money over time. Two things are required if you wish to consistently make money off into the future as an individual by virtue of your experience and wisdom. The first is wisdom. That is rare. The second is immortality. That is nonexistent.

Build your intellectual capital in your head and it dies with you. You (yes, you) will, sooner or later, die. Get over it. Manage to get your intellectual capital in more tangible form and it is transferable wherever and to whomever you wish. You might be able to share with your family how to continue to make money. You might even be able to take a vacation while you still are alive.

So... stop investing your precious time investigating an individual stock or idea. Start investing your time in developing your methodology. Don't make individual trades. Even if you're right, they are a one-time occurrence.

The next time you get a tout or great idea about what is going to move a particular stock up or down? Even if (ha!) you think it's a "sure thing"? Don't make the trade.

# "The Dog Ate My Analyst Report"

We have a dog named Brian (yes, named after the dog in "Family Guy"). Brian is good-natured and, by all we can tell, a fairly honest fellow.

Stock analysts? Have to think about that one. It has always struck us as strange that when a major bank's analyst pounds the table the stock gets a pop in price. Is today "Epiphany Day" for the analyst? Can their opinion really be of superior quality? Most studies find that analysts on average do no better than random... in fact— surprise, surprise—actually slightly worse. To top it off, intuitively speaking... How can 100 analysts from the top business schools all be right when they have differing opinions? Back to Lake Wobegone… all the children are above average.

There are some adviser services that try to identify "good" and "bad" analysts. A good idea but problematic in practice because the sample size is so small that statistically there is little information content in that differentiation.

It might be that Brian with all his honesty is at least random in his analysis. Thus, Brian should at least perform "average" right? Is something more sinister than analyst incompetence going on here?

Perhaps pounding the table is a way to get the next banking deal for the company. Perhaps the analyst is not saying what he or she really thinks. We can not know that for sure, let alone know the reasons. Nevertheless, we would prefer that Brian eat the analyst reports. In fact why stop there? Go ahead and eat the analyst too.

# Odds and Consequences

We tell our children consider not just the odds of an event but also the impact. Obviously don't worry about things with small odds of occurring and small consequences if they do. Obviously be concerned about things with large odds and big impact. But what about low odds but big impact? High odds but low impact?

Society focuses more on probability. What's not immediate is hard for (politicians and) us to stay with. We suggest however that impact (consequences) is more important. Events with cataclysmic consequences—even if unlikely—merit thought. If nothing's to be done, so be it. But if something can, it's worth your time.

The classic example: Pascal's Wager. The brilliant 17th-century mathematician Blaise Pascal reasoned a rational person should live as though God exists, not from faith, but mathematics. Do so? and God actually doesn't exist? You made a mistake. Lost pleasures. Do not? and God actually exists? You made a catastrophic mistake. Abandoned infinite gain, eternity in Heaven. Risk? Infinite loss, eternity in Hell. Groundbreaking probability and decision theory.

In investments, opportunities surround us to select probability (security is another name for it) over consequence. There are two forms of this: ignoring small probability huge impact and ignoring huge probability small negative impact. In the former case, activities such as writing naked options (colorfully referred to as "picking up nickels in front of a steamroller") win (return profit) most of the time, but occasionally dish out catastrophic loss. In the latter, "safe" government bonds (after tax and inflation) actually guarantee loss.

# Where No Man Has Gone Before

Quantum physics is above our pay grade. We struggled unsuccessfully with "A Brief History of Time" despite Hawking's assurance this is the simple version for us unwashed. Our understanding falters at infinity. It crash-lands around the Heisenberg Uncertainty Principle. We've a vague and highly unsettling concept along the lines of "the act of observing changes the event observed".

What has this to do with investing? We quickly go down the Rabbit Hole. What if the "empirical" knowledge of "objective reality" we so prize (and so diligently seek) is being mucked up by our very act of looking for it? Worse, if so, is it useless to try? Can we "sneak up" on the reality we seek? Observe it better from afar (whatever the heck that is) or more correctly if in some other way?

We've read quite a bit on this and related topics and so far find it unsatisfactory and/or inapplicable. We did however eventually reach an armed truce with our understanding of the Universe, which permits us to remain sane and continue to ply our trade with a reasonable expectation of success. For your continued entertainment here it is.

The question whether (a) *reality courteously re-aligns itself* to reflect our hard work in trying to act only from "empirical observation", or (b) our hard work *causes us to align* with an already-determined future "objective reality"…
Unfortunately both clauses still contain those two pesky words, "hard work"...

Therefore, back to it.  Hopefully better investors than theoretical physicists.

# Three-to-Two, or Timbuktu?

Last New England Fair of the year. Fryeburg, Maine. Watch leaves turn color and yes, horse racing. Urge on the pacers and trotters. Wonderland at ten years old. Money without effort? Oh my goodness! But Grandma needs to place our bets. Not Saratoga, or anything close. Betting is small, purse the same, but actual money. Billy Kid out of the Two position. Mediocre on paper. Morning line 10/1. Told we were good at math, we see him a 3/2 favorite. No way would we bet on this horse. We learn an investment lesson over the next two minutes and five seconds, when...

Billy Kid wins by a mile. What happened? The answer is, always has been, always will be, "We do not have to know. We only need know who knows". Not hard is it? Earlier we observed that we've no control over where the train goes. We only can hope to discern the intentions of those who do have some control. Nejat Seyhun wrote one of the better books on the subject, confirming statistically the predictive power of watching what "insiders" (officers, directors, large shareholders) do.

Yet... are there times when this doesn't work so well? When does Three-to-Two turn into Timbuktu? When consensus is too powerful. Saratoga, not Fryeburg Fair. Taking on analysts, who take on analysts, who do the same. NASDAQ in 2000. No "vig" there at all. Timbuktu. But follow the unfollowed. "Follow the money", as "Deep Throat" advised Woodward and Bernstein. Wise advice in any context. Watch the money, it usually does not lie. Insiders trade in one company of which they have expert knowledge and opinion.

Thank you Grandma, and thank you Billy Kid. The trainer shall be nameless.

# A One-Horse Race

How much fun would it be to arrive at a horse race and discover there's only one entry? We're sure it would be unexciting... and what about the betting crowd? How do we make money on this? And the purse money? We suppose the owner will get their entrance fee back, but that's about it. No fun for anyone. Even the horse will be bored (we think).

We've several examples of a complementary sort of thing that occurs... one that we rarely feel comfortable discussing. First, we have to take you back to Fryeburg Fair. Horse Race Number Three, seven entries, but not a sole runner has won a race this year... not a single one. Purse is $2,000. Not much, but something.

Thirty seconds before post. We notice something strange on the board. Saku, Number Four, getting strange win activity. He's getting bet hard. Too hard? Maybe not. Scurrying to the window, Saku is our bet. What next? We think you can guess.

Saku wins. Wire to wire!

The funny thing though is the winning time was pedestrian at best. As well, the normal rush you see in the home stretch at harness racing did not happen... almost as though the other drivers had no interest in winning... or could they have had an interest in winning by losing? No matter, that is not the main point.

Our main point is that harness horses are allowed to race through the age of fourteen. After that, forced retirement. Fryeburg Fair is the last fair of the year.

Clearly these were not great horses and only eligible for the fair circuit. Saku is fourteen years old. This is the gelding's last race of his life. Did the other drivers try, or did they just give him one? Who knew? Somebody, I assure you.

January 5th, 2002. Giants Stadium. A night game. Michael Strahan, playing for the Giants, is one sack away from the season sack record, held by Mark Gastineau, currently at 21.5 sacks.

Brett Favre, a well-known "colleague" of Strahan, is the Green Bay quarterback. Strahan may not get the sack record. There is only 2:46 left in the now-uncompetitive last game of the season. Favre under center. He knows the drill.

Favre spots Strahan moving to Favre's right side before the snap. Favre fakes a hand-off and goes right too. Inexplicably runs softly into Strahan. Strahan tackles him softly as well and Favre goes down. Gets up smiling. Mission accomplished. Mark Gastineau was upset with the fix for breaking his record, right? Nope, not at all. Mark was the first to give Michael a big hug after the game.

Former Giants coach Jim Fassel said, "If players have respect for that person, and he is close to breaking the record... I mean, you know, you've seen it in baseball, a guy is going to have a home-run record, an RBI record, if it doesn't matter to the game they'll put a fastball (down the middle) and let him knock it out of here. So if they have respect for the player, sometimes, I gonna let you get it."

What has all this to do with the corner of Wall and Broad streets? What do we learn from the gentleman's agreement?

Often what we call competitors are really colleagues. They cannot exist without each other. The Washington Generals, who are they? They are the Harlem Globetrotters' opponents in every game. The obligatory clowns. Wait... what would the Globetrotters do without the Generals? The Generals without the Globetrotters? They even ride on the same team bus!

This need for each other in the professional realm is common. The concept is called "repeat players". Realtors, lawyers who practice cooperation, the government (especially the government) and yes, of course Wall Street too. Never think that the banker or trader cares more about you than their purported competitor. The guy at UBS was out until the wee hours with the guy at Morgan. They know there are more transactions than yours.

You are not a member of the club. You are the customer. To be used by the club. If a price must be paid, the customer pays it. In entertainment, government, you name it. As an investor you are "buying the ticket." As in the horse race, late game sack, government market intervention, or real estate deal. The boys and girls in the club only take, they never pay.

As in the famous old story of the Wall Street visitor being shown the brokers' yachts, asks, "Where are the customers' yachts?"

# "Meet the Portfolio Managers"

Now a rare peek behind the scenes at a hedge fund "quant shop." The "back office." The guts of any investment house. Generating alpha. Making buy/sell decisions. Making money. One of the senior partners walks us around...

"We've discussed the dangers of being human. Successful portfolio managers, as in any field, risk developing outrageous egos and visiting at least two places we'd rather they didn't go. The first is a narcissism leading to cheating on your expense report, cheating on your spouse (worst with coworkers), demanding outlandish perqs and compensation, constant threat of quitting. The second risk is just becoming downright insufferable... the more successful, often the more arrogant, cocky, smart-alecky, autocratic, opinionated and inflexible.

"We've no solution to the second risk. I'm delighted, however, to assure you with near-absolute certainty that none of our portfolio managers are in danger of any of that first type of personality disorder.

"That is because they are software. These PMs have never demanded a corner office or sexually harassed a coworker. They produce pretty consistent results, delivering returns beating most of their competition. They've never asked for a vacation, overtime or even a raise. We thought you'd like to meet a few of them.

"The senior member of our team is Sam. Algorithm Sam was first implemented in 1996. Algorithm Sam was named in honor of our longtime friend Samuel Eisenstadt, co-founder and for decades Research Chairman of the Value Line

Investment Survey, perhaps the best known anomaly to the Efficient Market Hypothesis. Algorithm Sam runs our classic market-neutral stock portfolio 50 longs against 50 others short. Sam runs a tight ship, disciplined in the extreme, tolerates zero variation in process or procedure, teaches our younger PMs to do the same. Where he's completely inflexible about following the rules, he's very open-minded about developing them. He's neither a fundamental nor a technical guy. Another of Sam's strengths is his asymmetrical design: he knows different variables move stocks up as move them down.

"Next please say hello to Snow White. One of our real rock stars. She's boss of an eight-algorithm team including herself and seven diminutive gentlemen (Bashful, Happy, Sleepy, Dopey, Sneezy, Grumpy, Doc). Former coal miners all, these guys don't mind high risk! Get a kick from it. Each likes to pick just one or two big-cap stocks long and another couple short. Very concentrated portfolios. Individually these guys would wipe out. The volatility would kill them. Worse, they're not team players. They like the stock they like, don't give a whit whether their coworker doubles up. We'd not even give them the time of day were it not for Snow White. She's a wise mistress, allocating capital and risk among her team masterfully.

"Our newest PM is Max. He trades broad themes (asset classes, countries, sectors, extreme big-caps) against each other, often using ETFs. Risk is Max's middle name. (Actually, he has no middle name; his given name is Maximum Drawdown). Max tries to find differences in indices or markets that already are extremely diversified so as to avoid his surname-sake. Max is managing his first allocation with us, a fresh-faced kid straight out of algorithm school.

"All of our managers act within our investment dogma: market neutrality, uncorrelated diversification, etc.

"Which brings us last (very much not least!) to Harry. Not on the payroll, just here in spirit every day. You know our respect—awe—for Harry Markowitz. The Magician. Harry taught us and the whole world about 'the only free lunch in investing' otherwise known as non-correlated diversification. We call it Something from Nothing. Harry is the reason we employ more than one portfolio manager and always will. The reason we do not even try to develop a single 'best' investment. Harry taught us that the perfect is a combination of the imperfect.

"Too, we've had to let a few managers go. Broke our hearts to see promising youngsters like Levi (The Leviathan) or Slim (Pickins) flame out, but despite their entreaties ('Put me in coach! I'm ready!') they were not ready. The out-of-sample testing was so promising, but it was not complete. We should have said no. Our fault. But these kids paid with their careers. Being the boss isn't all fun and games.

"Nor is it fun when your portfolio manager is not just algorithmic but also an insufferable, stubborn, inflexible, sarcastic, pompous know-it-all. All the more irritating when it's usually right. If we have a bad quarter and I demand to know what they plan to do about it, their stony contemptuous silence upbraids me. 'Get a grip on yourself, would you please? Stop whining. Haven't I always been right before? Go clean up. You're a mess. I liked our longs before. I like them better now. Our shorts were dogs. They're still dogs. I will make no changes to this portfolio. None. Zero. Zip. Nada. Do you understand? Quit sniveling and just Man Up, would you please? And close the door on your way out.'"

# Life after Debt?

Statistically speaking, and contrary to most thought, short interest is a rather significant indicator of future performance, but not as you might think. Talking heads on the Business Channel claim short interest means pent up buying power...when the evil shorts are forced to run for (to) cover, the stock will fly! Sometimes that happens...but on the margin quite the opposite occurs. We've asked the question previously and will ask again: on whom would you rather bet? Long only Mutual Fund types who do "Funnymental" investing with institutional money, or Hedge Fund types investing their own money? Prey or shark? I'd go with shark. Short interest is actually a good negative indicator, confirmed by numerous academic studies.

There is however one exception. Short interest related to a convertible bond. When a convertible is issued, it can represent a large portion of the market capitalization. Hedge funds go to work and do their thing. What is their thing? Buy the bond and remove the underlying stock risk by shorting the underlying stock. Presto! they have an "arbitrage" position. So there's your exception. Hedge funds shorting a stock not because of an opinion on the stock, but simply to hedge away risk from a convertible bond they bought. Again confirmed by good academic studies. Phew!

What about the studies that back up the general concept without reference to the convertible bond association? That means those studies have one big "Blind Spot". Or did the analyst get "Caught Looking"? Either way he struck out on his analysis. Yes Dorothy, there is life after debt... as long as the debt is a convertible bond.

# Goldilocks and the Three Bears

Once upon a time... there were three Bears.

A great, big, strapping Papa Bear. A sweet, nurturing, emotional Momma Bear. And little tiny, nerdy, intellectual Baby Bear.

All three Bears were convinced the market was overvalued. In short (get it?) all three Bears were, well, Bearish on the market.

Papa Bear was in fact known far and wide for his negative view of equities. No one could recall a time when Papa Bear had a Bullish view. Behind his back, the other animals referred to him as a "Perma-Bear". Papa boasted of having correctly called the stock market crashes of 1987 and 2000 as well as the financial crisis of 2008. The other animals dismissed this, pointing out—correctly—that Papa also had called crashes that did not materialize. Truth be told, Papa was always predicting another crash. "You called 18 of the last 3 crashes!" they taunted, laughing, "Even a stopped clock is right twice a day!"

Momma Bear was more collaborative and circumspect. Momma talked with her friends in the neighborhood investing club. She listened religiously to Suze Orman and, frankly, always was worried. Her anxiety knew no bounds. She worried for the future of her family. She fell prey to every scare-tactic and security-oriented scam thrown at her, on television and through the mail. The Bears' garage groaned with survivalist food. Their back yard garden was a welter of buried boxes of precious coins.

131

Both Papa and Momma had significantly underperformed the market. Pretty much forever. Despite the fact that Papa pulled down a very nice salary as a middle manager for a regulatory agency, they were just not getting ahead. Papa and Momma both worried obsessively that their Golden Years might have to be spent at the zoo, suffering the indignities of posing for pictures with small children. No one to wash the disgusting sticky ice cream out of their fur. Or worse. Far worse. They didn't want to think about it.

Baby Bear however was one very focused, tight-sphinctered little Bear. He had been to college. He not only did not sleep through Statistics class, he majored in it! Baby's dorm room had not movie star posters but pictures of Harry Markowitz, Ben Graham and David Dodd. When all the other bears in his fraternity were out drinking and chasing sorority bears, Baby Bear was up in his room re-reading *The Black Swan* by Nassim Taleb and *This Time is Different* by Carmen Reinhart and Kenneth Rogoff. Both copies were dogeared and heavily highlighted. He had never been to a rock concert, felt entertainment in general—and watching television in particular—a waste of time. His dream was someday to attend a lecture by Harry Markowitz and somehow be able to actually meet him afterward.

Baby Bear was a disciplined investor in the extreme. He bought low-cost index funds, engaged in a little market-neutral stock-picking arbitrage, bought a few private investments from people he knew very well and trusted. Baby was extraordinarily well diversified. Baby's one indulgence to his very Bearish nature were out-of-the-money index puts, which Baby bought and rolled over quarterly. Occasionally in a crash they paid off nicely, but most of the time they expired worthless, a 100% loss. Baby was unfazed. They were his insurance. He regarded them as a cost of doing business.

One of Baby Bear's classmates in business school was a very smart young woman named Goldilocks.

Goldilocks was a looker. On graduation Baby took a job in the quant shop at a high frequency trader, while Goldilocks became a night and weekend reporter for the local television affiliate. She worked long hours and reported incisively no matter how banal the assignment.

In no time Goldilocks had her own prime-time national network show and anchored the Business Channel. From this lofty perch Goldilocks aggressively made equity ownership accessible, understandable (and very profitable!) for the masses. She waged permanent (and largely unsuccessful) guerrilla wars... trying to keep both grandstanding anti-capitalist politicians and her own producers' slimy advertising products off of her show.

Baby Bear was a frequent and popular guest. He never quite got over the time Goldilocks surprised him with another guest. A most gracious Harry Markowitz had to shoulder most of the interview while Baby just stared in unbelieving awe, the autographed copy of one of Harry's books reverently unopened to this day.

Goldilocks and Baby Bear remained lifelong the closest of friends.

Baby was able to take very good care of his aging parents.

The subject of the zoo never was mentioned again.